CYBER SECURITY OPERATIONAL TECHNOLOGY BEST PRACTICE

TABLE OF CONTENTS

CYBER SECURITY OVERVIEW

1. WHAT IS CYBER OPERATIONAL TECHNOLOGY (OT)

Cyber Operational Technology (OT) refers to the systems and devices that are used to control and monitor physical processes in industries such as manufacturing, power generation, and transportation. These systems are often connected to the internet, making them vulnerable to cyber attacks. OT systems are typically not designed with cybersecurity in mind and can be more difficult to secure than traditional IT systems. As such, the security of OT systems is becoming an increasingly important concern, as cyber attacks on these systems can have severe consequences, such as physical damage to equipment or disruption of essential services.

ICS stands for Industrial Control Systems. These systems are used to control industrial processes and infrastructure such as power plants, water treatment facilities, and transportation systems.

ICS equipment includes devices such as programmable logic controllers (PLCs), human-machine interfaces (HMIs), and remote terminal units (RTUs) which are used to control and monitor industrial processes. These systems are also known as Supervisory Control and Data Acquisition (SCADA) systems.

A Programmable Logic Controller (PLC) is a type of computer-based industrial control system that can be programmed to perform a wide variety of control and automation tasks. These tasks can include monitoring and controlling industrial processes, machinery, and equipment, as well as communicating with other systems and devices. PLCs are commonly used in manufacturing, assembly, and other industrial settings to automate repetitive tasks, improve efficiency, and reduce human intervention. They are also used in building automation systems and transportation systems, such as elevators and conveyor systems. PLCs are typically programmed using specialized software, and they can be configured to communicate with other systems and devices using a variety of protocols, such as Ethernet, Modbus, and Profinet.

2. HISTORY OF CYBER SECURITY OPERATIONAL TECHNOLOGY THREAT

- The history of cyber threats to operational technology (OT) dates back to the early days of industrial control systems (ICS), which were first used in the 1970s. However, these early systems were not connected to the internet and were therefore not vulnerable to cyber attacks.
- As industrial control systems evolved and became more connected to the internet, they began to be targeted by cyber criminals. One of the earliest and most notable examples of this occurred in 2000, when the "ILOVEYOU" worm caused widespread damage to industrial control systems, including those used in power plants and water treatment facilities.
- In 2010, the Stuxnet worm was discovered and caused significant damage to the Iranian nuclear program by targeting industrial control systems used in the country's uranium enrichment facilities. This was

one of the first known examples of a cyber-attack being used to cause physical damage to equipment.

- In 2017, the WannaCry ransomware attack affected a number of industrial organizations, including a UK hospital and a German steel mill, by encrypting their data and demanding a ransom to restore access.
- In 2020, the Triton malware was discovered, which targeted industrial control systems in the Middle East. The malware was designed to cause physical damage to equipment by manipulating the systems that control the operation of the equipment. This incident highlighted the growing concern of the potential consequences of cyber attacks on operational technology.
- These examples demonstrate the increasing sophistication of cyber threats to operational technology and the potential for these attacks to cause significant damage to equipment and disruption of essential services. Due to the critical nature of these systems and the potential consequences of a successful attack, the security of operational technology is becoming an increasingly important concern for organizations and governments around the world.

3. WHAT IS CYBER OPERATIONAL TECHNOLOGY (OT) COMMON THREATS?

There are several common threats to Cyber Operational Technology (OT) systems, including:

1. Ransomware: This is a type of malware that encrypts a victim's data and demands a ransom to restore access. Ransomware can cause significant disruption to operations and potentially lead to a loss of data.

2. Advanced Persistent Threats (APTs): APTs are highly sophisticated cyber attacks that are typically carried out by nation-states or well-funded criminal groups. These attacks are designed to infiltrate a system

and remain undetected for long periods of time, allowing attackers to steal sensitive data or disrupt operations.

3. Industrial Control System (ICS) malware: This type of malware is specifically designed to target industrial control systems and can cause physical damage to equipment or disrupt essential services. Examples of ICS malware include Stuxnet and Triton.
4. Phishing: Phishing is a technique used to trick individuals into revealing sensitive information, such as login credentials, by disguising a malicious link or attachment as something legitimate.
5. Unpatched software: Many OT systems are using outdated software which is not updated regularly, making it vulnerable to known vulnerabilities that have been identified and patched.
6. Insufficient access controls: Many OT systems do not have sufficient access controls in place, making it easy for an attacker to gain unauthorized access to the system.
7. Remote access vulnerabilities: Many OT systems are remotely accessible, making them vulnerable to cyber attacks if proper security measures are not in place.
8. Lack of monitoring and incident response: Many organizations do not have adequate monitoring and incident response capabilities in place to detect and respond to cyber threats to their OT systems.

These are just a few examples of the common threats to OT systems, and the security landscape is constantly evolving. It is essential for organizations to stay informed about the latest cyber threats and to implement appropriate security measures to protect their OT systems.

4. WHAT IS CYBER OPERATIONAL TECHNOLOGY (OT) COMMON PORTS AT RISK AND BEST PRACTICE?

There are several common ports that are used by Cyber Operational Technology (OT) systems and are at risk of being targeted by cyber attackers. Some of these ports include:

1. TCP Port 502: This port is commonly used for communication between programmable logic controllers (PLCs) and other industrial control systems (ICS) devices. It is often used for Modbus protocol, which is widely used in the industrial sector.
2. TCP and UDP Port 161: This port is commonly used for Simple Network Management Protocol (SNMP) communication, which is used to monitor and control network devices.
3. TCP Port 80 and 443: These ports are commonly used for web-based communication, and are often used to access human-machine interfaces (HMIs) and other web-based applications that are used to control and monitor industrial systems.
4. TCP and UDP Port 8888: This port is commonly used for communication between ICS devices and remote management servers, as well as data exchange between ICS devices.
5. TCP and UDP Port 47808: This port is commonly used for communication between ICS devices and remote management servers, and for data exchange between ICS devices.

To protect these ports and the systems that use them, best practices include:

1. Segmenting the OT network from the IT network to limit the ability of an attacker to move laterally within the network.
2. Implementing network security devices, such as firewalls and intrusion detection/prevention systems, to monitor and control access to the OT network.
3. Regularly monitoring and analyzing network traffic to detect and respond to potential threats.

4. Regularly patching and updating software and firmware to address known vulnerabilities.
5. Implementing strong authentication and access controls to prevent unauthorized access to the OT network.
6. Conducting regular security assessments and penetration testing to identify vulnerabilities and weaknesses in the OT network.
7. Regularly training employees on security best practices and how to recognize and respond to potential cyber threats.
8. Having an incident response plan in place to quickly and effectively respond to security incidents.

TOP ICS PROTOCOLS THAT COULD BE SUSCEPTIBLE TO CYBER THREAT

Industrial control systems (ICS) protocols are used to communicate between devices and equipment in industrial environments. These protocols are often proprietary and unencrypted, which makes them vulnerable to cyber threats. Some of the top ICS protocols that are susceptible to cyber threats include:

- Modbus: A widely used communication protocol in industrial control systems, but it is unencrypted and has no built-in security features.
- DNP3 (Distributed Network Protocol): This protocol is used in the electric utility industry for the supervision of substation automation and remote terminal units (RTUs). It is unencrypted, making it vulnerable to cyber attacks.
- SCADA (Supervisory Control and Data Acquisition) : This protocol is used to monitor and control industrial processes and infrastructure, such as power plants and manufacturing facilities. It is also unencrypted and has no built-in security features.

- OLE for Process Control (OPC) : OPC is a standard for data exchange between Windows applications and industrial devices. However, it does not have any built-in security features, making it vulnerable to cyber attacks.
- S7 Communications: This protocol is used to communicate between PLCs and devices in industrial environments. It is unencrypted, making it vulnerable to cyber attacks.
- Ethernet/IP: A popular industrial Ethernet protocol used in control and automation systems.
- Profinet: A real-time Ethernet protocol used in industrial automation systems.
- OPC UA: An open standard for secure and reliable data exchange in industrial automation systems.
- DNP3: A communications protocol used in the electric utility industry for the supervision of substation automation and remote terminal units (RTUs)
- IEC60870-5-104: A communication protocol used in electric utility substation automation systems.
- It's important to note that these protocols are often used in critical infrastructure and the consequences of a successful cyber attack could be severe. Therefore, it's important to implement a robust security strategy to protect these protocols and the systems that use them.

To protect these OT ports, best practices include:

- -Segmenting the ICS network from the IT network to prevent unauthorized access
- -Monitoring and logging all network traffic for suspicious activity
- -Restricting access to OT ports to only authorized personnel

- -Using firewalls and intrusion detection/prevention systems to block unauthorized access
- -Keeping software and systems up to date with the latest security patches
- -Implementing a vulnerability management program to identify and address vulnerabilities in a timely manner.

It's also important to have regular security audits and penetration testing to identify and address vulnerabilities and to train employees to be aware of potential security risks and how to identify and report them.

By following these best practices, organizations can better protect their OT systems and reduce the risk of a successful cyber attack.

1. WHAT IS CYBER OPERATIONAL TECHNOLOGY (OT) COMMON IOC?

Cyber Operational Technology (OT) refers to the use of technology in industrial control systems (ICS) and other critical infrastructure environments. Indicators of compromise (IOCs) are signs that a system or network has been compromised by a cyber attacker. Common IOCs in the OT environment include:

1. Unusual network traffic: Traffic patterns that deviate from normal behavior, such as an increase in traffic to a specific IP address, could indicate an attempted attack.
2. Unusual process behavior: Changes in the behavior of a process or device, such as a sudden change in temperature or pressure, could indicate a compromise.
3. Unusual system activity: Changes in system behavior, such as unexpected shutdowns or restarts, could indicate a compromise.
4. Unusual user activity: Unusual login attempts or user actions, such as access to sensitive data, could indicate a compromise.

5. Unusual files or software: The presence of unknown or unauthorized files or software on a system could indicate a compromise.
6. Unusual system configurations: Changes in system configurations, such as new users or new network connections, could indicate a compromise.
7. Unusual log entries: Entries in system logs that deviate from normal behavior, such as failed login attempts or system errors, could indicate a compromise.

It's important to regularly monitor for these and other IOCs to detect potential breaches and take appropriate action to mitigate them. Additionally, it's important to have a incident response plan in place to quickly identify and respond to security breaches.

2. WHAT IS CYBER OPERATIONAL TECHNOLOGY (OT) REFERENCE ARCHITECTURE

A Cyber Operational Technology (OT) reference architecture is a framework that outlines the components, relationships, and interactions of the various systems and technologies involved in securing industrial control systems (ICS) and other critical infrastructure environments. The reference architecture provides a holistic view of the security landscape and helps organizations to better understand and address the unique challenges of securing these systems.

A typical Cyber OT reference architecture includes the following components:

1. Security controls: This includes firewalls, intrusion detection/prevention systems, and other security devices that are used to protect the OT environment.
2. Network segmentation: This involves dividing the OT network into different segments to prevent unauthorized access and to isolate critical systems and data.

3. Monitoring and logging: This includes the collection and analysis of data from various sources, such as network traffic, system logs, and device sensors, to detect security breaches and anomalies.
4. Access control: This includes the use of authentication and encryption to secure communications and to restrict access to only authorized personnel.
5. Patch management: This includes the implementation of a process for keeping software and systems up-to-date with the latest security patches.
6. Vulnerability management: This includes the identification and management of vulnerabilities in the OT environment, such as software and system vulnerabilities, to prevent breaches.
7. Incident response: This includes the development of a plan for quickly identifying and responding to security breaches.
8. Employee training: This includes training employees to be aware of potential security risks and how to identify and report them.

The reference architecture should be flexible enough to adapt to the specific needs of an organization, taking into account the unique characteristics of the environment, such as the type of technology used and the threat landscape.

3. WHAT IS CYBER OPERATIONAL TECHNOLOGY (OT) SECURITY LAYERS

Cyber Operational Technology (OT) security layers refer to the different levels of protection that are used to secure industrial control systems (ICS) and other critical infrastructure environments. These layers work together to create a comprehensive security strategy that addresses the unique challenges of securing OT systems.

The common security layers of Cyber OT are:

1. Perimeter security: This layer includes firewalls, intrusion detection/prevention systems, and other security devices that are used to protect the OT environment from external threats.
2. Network segmentation: This layer involves dividing the OT network into different segments to prevent unauthorized access and to isolate critical systems and data. This can be achieved through the use of VLANs, VPNs, and other segmentation methods.
3. Device security: This layer includes the use of security features, such as encryption, authentication, and access controls, to secure devices and equipment in the OT environment.
4. Monitoring and logging: This layer includes the collection and analysis of data from various sources, such as network traffic, system logs, and device sensors, to detect security breaches and anomalies.
5. Vulnerability management: This layer includes the identification and management of vulnerabilities in the OT environment, such as software and system vulnerabilities, to prevent breaches.
6. Incident response: This layer includes the development of a plan for quickly identifying and responding to security breaches.
7. Compliance: This layer includes the implementation of compliance requirements and standards, such as NIST SP 800-82, NIST SP 800-53, IEC 62443, and ISO 27001, to ensure that the organization's security practices are in line with industry standards.
8. Training and Awareness: This layer includes training employees to be aware of potential security risks and how to identify and report them.

Implementing multiple layers of security provides a defense-in-depth approach that helps to ensure that the OT environment is protected against a wide range of threats. Each layer provides a different level of protection and addresses different types of threats, making it more difficult for an attacker to penetrate the system.

4. WHAT IS CYBER OPERATIONAL TECHNOLOGY (OT) NETWORK SEGMENTATION BEST PRACTICE?

Cyber Operational technology (OT) network segmentation is the process of dividing a computer network into smaller subnetworks in order to improve security, performance, and manageability. Best practice for OT network segmentation includes:

1. Defining clear boundaries between different segments of the network, such as between production and non-production areas.
2. Implementing strict access controls to limit access to sensitive areas of the network.
3. Using firewalls, intrusion detection and prevention systems, and other security measures to protect the network from unauthorized access and attacks.
4. Regularly monitoring and reviewing network activity to detect and respond to security threats.

5. Segmenting the network using VLAN and firewall, implementing access control list, and using network monitoring tools.
6. Segmenting the network physically and logically.
7. Use of micro-segmentation to secure the communication between different segments of the network.
8. Implementing security policies, procedures and guidelines to govern the access and use of network resources.
9. Regularly testing the network to identify vulnerabilities and implement security patches as needed.
10. Continuously monitoring and analyzing network traffic to detect and prevent cyber threats in real-time.

5. WHAT IS CYBER OPERATIONAL TECHNOLOGY (OT) RISK MANAGEMENT BEST PRACTICE?

Cyber Operational technology (OT) risk management best practice involves identifying, assessing, and mitigating the potential risks that could impact the availability, integrity, and confidentiality of industrial control systems and other operational technology assets. Some best practices for OT risk management include:

1. Conducting a comprehensive risk assessment to identify and prioritize potential risks to the OT environment.
2. Developing a risk management plan that outlines specific actions to be taken to mitigate identified risks.
3. Implementing security controls, such as firewalls, intrusion detection systems, and access controls, to protect against cyber threats.
4. Regularly monitoring and reviewing network activity to detect and respond to security threats.

5. Establishing incident response and business continuity plans to minimize the impact of a security incident.
6. Regularly testing and updating security controls to ensure they are functioning properly and are up-to-date with the latest threat information.
7. Developing and implementing security policies and procedures to govern the access and use of OT systems and data.
8. Establishing training and awareness programs to educate employees about cyber risks and best practices for protecting against them.
9. Continuously monitoring and analyzing network traffic to detect and prevent cyber threats in real-time.
10. Building an incident response team that is dedicated to identifying, responding to, and mitigating cyber threats to the OT environment.

6. WHAT IS CYBER OPERATIONAL TECHNOLOGY (OT) ZERO TRUST ARCHITECTURE?

What is Cyber Operational technology (OT) zero trust architecture

A zero-trust architecture is a security model that assumes that all network traffic is untrusted, regardless of whether it originates from inside or outside the network perimeter. In Cyber Operational technology (OT) zero trust architecture, it involves applying the principle of least privilege, where only the minimum level of access required to perform a task is granted. It also involves implementing strict access controls and continuous monitoring to identify and prevent unauthorized access or malicious activity on the network.

Some key elements of a zero trust architecture in the OT environment include:

1. Micro-segmentation: This involves dividing the network into smaller, isolated segments to limit the scope of a security incident.

2. Identity and access management: This involves verifying the identity of all users and devices and enforcing strict access controls to limit access to sensitive areas of the network.
3. Multi-factor authentication: This involves requiring multiple forms of authentication, such as a password and a security token, to access the network.
4. Continuous monitoring and threat detection: This involves monitoring network traffic in real-time to identify and respond to potential security threats.
5. Encryption: This involves encrypting all sensitive data to protect it from unauthorized access.
6. Network isolation: This involves physically isolating critical systems, such as control systems, from the rest of the network to protect them from cyber threats.
7. Regularly testing, monitoring, and updating security controls to stay current with the latest threats.
8. Risk management approach: This involves identifying, assessing, and mitigating the potential risks that could impact the availability, integrity, and confidentiality of industrial control systems and other operational technology assets.
9. Regularly monitoring and reviewing network activity to detect and respond to security threats.
10. Developing and implementing security policies, procedures, and guidelines to govern the access and use of network resources.

7. WHAT IS CYBER OPERATIONAL TECHNOLOGY (OT) CLOUD SECURITY BEST PRACTICE?

Cybersecurity best practices for Operational Technology (OT) in the cloud include:

1. Implementing secure network segmentation to isolate OT systems and networks from the rest of the organization's IT systems and networks.
2. Ensuring that all cloud-based OT systems and applications are patched and updated regularly to address known vulnerabilities.
3. Implementing multi-factor authentication for all access to cloud-based OT systems and applications.
4. Implementing a robust incident response plan to quickly detect, contain, and recover from cyber incidents.
5. Regularly monitoring and analyzing network traffic for abnormal activity and anomalies.
6. Conducting regular penetration testing to identify vulnerabilities and weaknesses in cloud-based OT systems and applications.
7. Implementing data encryption to protect sensitive information in transit and at rest.
8. Regularly training employees on cybersecurity best practices and creating a culture of security.
9. Implementing a cloud access security broker (CASB) solution to monitor and control access to cloud-based resources.
10. Regularly testing backup and disaster recovery plans to ensure that they are effective in the event of a cyber incident.

8. WHAT IS CYBER OPERATIONAL TECHNOLOGY (OT) IDENTIFY ACCESS MANAGEMENT BEST PRACTICE

- Cybersecurity best practices for Operational Technology (OT) identity and access management include:
- Implementing a strict least privilege model for access to OT systems and applications, ensuring that only authorized personnel have access to the information and resources they need to perform their jobs.
- Implementing multi-factor authentication for all access to OT systems and applications, including remote access.
- Regularly reviewing and revoking access rights for employees and contractors who no longer need access to OT systems and applications.
- Implementing role-based access control (RBAC) to ensure that access to OT systems and applications is based on an individual's job function and responsibilities.
- Implementing a centralized identity and access management system that allows for the management of user accounts, groups, and access rights across all OT systems and applications.
- Regularly monitoring and auditing access to OT systems and applications to detect and prevent unauthorized access.
- Implementing security controls such as firewalls, intrusion detection and prevention systems, and network segmentation to protect OT systems and applications from unauthorized access.
- Regularly training employees on cybersecurity best practices, including password management and the proper handling of sensitive information.
- Implementing an incident response plan to quickly detect and respond to any incidents of unauthorized access.
- Regularly testing and updating security controls to ensure that they are able to detect and prevent the latest threats.

9. WHAT IS CYBER OPERATIONAL TECHNOLOGY (OT) COMMON CYBER FRAMEWORKS?

There are several common cyber frameworks that organizations can use to improve their cybersecurity posture for Operational Technology (OT) systems and networks. These include:

1. NIST Cybersecurity Framework (CSF): Developed by the National Institute of Standards and Technology (NIST), the CSF provides a flexible and adaptable approach to managing cybersecurity risks and is widely used across a variety of industries.
2. IEC 62443: Developed by the International Electrotechnical Commission (IEC), this standard provides guidelines for securing industrial control systems (ICS) and other OT systems.
3. ISA/IEC 62443: This standard provides a comprehensive set of guidelines for securing industrial control systems (ICS) and other OT systems.
4. NERC CIP: Developed by the North American Electric Reliability Corporation (NERC), the Critical Infrastructure Protection (CIP) standards provide a set of guidelines for protecting critical infrastructure in the electric power industry.
5. ISO 27001: Developed by the International Organization for Standardization (ISO), this standard provides a framework for managing information security and is widely used in a variety of industries.
6. COBIT: Developed by ISACA, Control Objectives for Information and related Technology (COBIT) is an IT governance framework that can be used to improve the management of IT in an organization.
7. SANS Critical Security Control (CSC) : Developed by the SANS Institute, the CSC provides a set of guidelines for identifying, assessing, and mitigating the most critical cybersecurity risks facing an organization.

8. SOC 2: Developed by the AICPA, SOC 2 is a set of guidelines for evaluating the security, availability, processing integrity, confidentiality, and privacy of a service organization's system and controls.

These frameworks provide guidelines and best practices for identifying, assessing, and mitigating cybersecurity risks, and help organizations to improve their overall cybersecurity posture.

10. WHAT IS CYBER OPERATIONAL TECHNOLOGY (OT) VULNERABILITY MANAGEMENT BEST PRACTICE?

Cybersecurity best practices for vulnerability management in Operational Technology (OT) systems and networks include:

1. Regularly identifying and assessing vulnerabilities in OT systems and networks, including software, hardware, and firmware vulnerabilities.
2. Prioritizing vulnerabilities based on their potential impact and likelihood of being exploited.
3. Implementing remediation measures to address identified vulnerabilities, such as applying software patches, configuring security controls, or replacing outdated equipment.
4. Establishing a vulnerability management program that includes regular scanning, testing, and monitoring to detect new vulnerabilities as they arise.
5. Keeping software and firmware versions updated and patched with the latest security updates and patches.
6. Regularly monitoring and analyzing network traffic for abnormal activity and anomalies.
7. Conducting regular penetration testing to identify vulnerabilities and weaknesses in cloud-based OT systems and applications.

8. Regularly testing backup and disaster recovery plans to ensure that they are effective in the event of a cyber incident.
9. Implementing incident response plans and procedures to quickly detect, respond, and recover from security incidents.
10. Regularly training employees and contractors on cybersecurity best practices and creating a culture of security.
11. Developing a continuous monitoring approach, where vulnerabilities are continuously identified, assessed, and mitigated over time, rather than a one-time or periodic approach.
12. Collaborating with vendors and third-party service providers to ensure that their products and services are secure and free from vulnerabilities

11. CHANGE MANAGEMENT BEST PRACTICE FOR OPERATION TECHNOLOGY

Change management best practices for Operation Technology (OT) include:

1. Risk Assessment: Conduct a risk assessment to identify and evaluate the potential impact of the change on the organization's OT systems and processes.

2. Communication Plan: Develop a communication plan to ensure that all stakeholders are informed of the change, its rationale, and its impact on their work.
3. Impact Analysis: Conduct an impact analysis to identify the potential impact of the change on the organization's operations, including any potential disruptions, and to develop a plan to mitigate these impacts.
4. Test and Validation: Test and validate the change in a controlled environment to ensure that it will function as intended and to identify and address any issues before it is implemented in production.
5. Training: Provide training to the personnel who will be affected by the change so that they understand the new processes and procedures and are able to effectively support the change.
6. Rollback Plan: Develop a rollback plan to quickly and effectively revert to the previous state in case of any issues with the change.
7. Incident management: Develop an incident management plan that includes communication, escalation, and resolution procedures for addressing any issues that arise after the change is implemented.
8. Monitoring: Monitor the change after it is implemented to ensure that it is functioning as intended and to identify and address any issues.
9. Continuous improvement: Continuously monitor and assess the effectiveness of the change management process and make improvements as necessary.
10. Report: Provide a report to the management that includes the findings, recommendations, and mitigation plan.

Overall, change management for OT systems is critical to ensure that changes are implemented in a controlled and predictable manner, minimizing the risk of disruptions to operations and ensuring the continued safe and secure operation of critical systems. By following best practices and regularly monitoring and assessing the effectiveness of the change management process, organizations can minimize the risk of disruptions and ensure the continued safe and secure operation of their OT systems.

12. WHAT IS CYBER OPERATIONAL TECHNOLOGY (OT) INDUSTRIAL DMZ BEST PRACTICE?

A Cyber Operational Technology (OT) industrial DMZ (Demilitarized Zone) is a network architecture that separates the operational technology network, which controls industrial processes and equipment, from the IT network, which handles information and communications. The best practice for implementing an OT industrial DMZ is to physically separate the two networks using a firewall and to limit communication between the networks to only the necessary protocols and ports. Additionally, it is recommended to monitor and log all traffic between the networks, to implement security controls such as intrusion detection and prevention systems, and to regularly conduct vulnerability assessments and penetration testing.

13. WHAT IS CYBER OPERATIONAL TECHNOLOGY (OT) THREAT PROFILING BEST PRACTICE?

Cyber Operational Technology (OT) threat profiling is the process of identifying and analyzing potential security threats to industrial control systems and critical infrastructure. Best practices for OT threat profiling include:

1. Identifying and analyzing the assets, systems, and processes that are critical to the organization's operations.
2. Understanding the attack vectors and methods that are commonly used against industrial control systems, such as phishing, malware, and network scanning.
3. Identifying potential vulnerabilities in the systems and processes, such as outdated software, weak passwords, and lack of network segmentation.

4. Developing a risk management plan that includes measures to mitigate or eliminate identified threats, such as implementing security controls, developing incident response plans, and conducting regular security assessments and audits.
5. Continuously monitoring and updating the threat profile as new threats and vulnerabilities are identified.
6. Regularly training employees on security best practices and incident response procedures
7. Evaluating third party vendors and maintaining a robust vendor management program.
8. Having incident response plan in place and regular testing of incident response plans.
9. Collaborating with other organizations and industry groups to share threat intelligence and best practices.

14. WHAT IS CYBER OPERATIONAL TECHNOLOGY (OT) BEST PRACTICES TO SELECT SIEM MONITORING?

Cyber Operational Technology (OT) best practices for selecting a Security Information and Event Management (SIEM) system include:

1. Assessing the organization's specific needs and requirements, such as the type and number of devices and systems that need to be monitored, the level of security and compliance that is required, and the level of customization and integration that is needed.
2. Evaluating the SIEM system's capability to collect and analyze data from different types of devices and systems, such as industrial control systems, SCADA systems, and IT systems.

3. Evaluating the system's ability to detect and alert on security events in real-time and its capability of storing historical data for forensic and compliance purposes.
4. Considering the scalability and flexibility of the SIEM system to adapt to the organization's changing needs and to integrate with other security tools.
5. Verifying the vendor's expertise and experience in providing SIEM solutions for industrial control systems and OT environments.
6. Evaluating the vendor's track record for providing timely updates and support in case of any security incidents.
7. Evaluating the system's ability to detect and respond to advanced threats and targeted attacks.
8. Assessing if SIEM solution provides visibility and control over third-party vendors and remote access.
9. Verifying the compliance of the SIEM system with industry standards and regulations, such as NIST, IEC62443 and others.

15. WHAT IS CYBER OPERATIONAL TECHNOLOGY (OT) BEST PRACTICE TO SELECT MDR SOLUTION?

Cyber Operational Technology (OT) best practices for selecting a Managed Detection and Response (MDR) solution include:

1. Assessing the organization's specific needs and requirements, such as the type and number of devices and systems that need to be monitored, the level of security and compliance that is required, and the level of customization and integration that is needed.
2. Evaluating the MDR solution's capability to collect and analyze data from different types of devices and systems, such as industrial control systems, SCADA systems, and IT systems.
3. Verifying the vendor's expertise and experience in providing MDR solutions for industrial control systems and OT environments.
4. Evaluating the system's ability to detect and respond to advanced threats and targeted attacks.

5. Verifying the MDR solution's compliance with industry standards and regulations, such as NIST, IEC62443 and others.
6. Considering the scalability and flexibility of the MDR solution to adapt to the organization's changing needs and to integrate with other security tools.
7. Assessing the vendor's track record for providing timely updates and support in case of any security incidents.
8. Evaluating the system's ability to provide detailed incident reports and forensic analysis
9. Assessing if MDR solution provides visibility and control over third-party vendors and remote access.
10. Verifying if MDR solution includes regular testing, training and drill of incident response plans.
11. Evaluating the vendor's incident response capabilities, including the availability of security experts and incident response teams.
12. Considering the cost of the solution and the level of service provided by the vendor.

16. WHAT ARE THE COMMON DEVICES AND LAYERS OF OPERATIONAL TECHNOLOGY (OT)

Operational Technology (OT) refers to the systems, devices, and networks that are used to control and monitor industrial processes and equipment. Common devices and layers of OT include:

1. Field devices: These include sensors, actuators, and other devices that are connected to the process or equipment being controlled. Examples include temperature sensors, flow meters, and valve actuators.

2. Control systems: These include programmable logic controllers (PLCs), distributed control systems (DCSs), and supervisory control and data acquisition (SCADA) systems. These systems receive input from the field devices and use that information to control the process or equipment.
3. Network infrastructure: This includes the communication networks and protocols that connect the field devices and control systems to the rest of the organization's IT systems. Examples include Ethernet, Modbus, and Profinet.
4. Human-Machine Interface (HMI): These are the graphical interfaces that operators use to interact with the control systems and view process data.
5. IT systems: These include the IT systems that support the organization's operations, such as enterprise resource planning (ERP) systems, manufacturing execution systems (MES), and data historians.
6. Cloud-Based services: These include the cloud-based services that support the organization's operations such as asset management, predictive maintenance, remote monitoring and control.
7. Mobile devices: These include mobile devices that are used by operators to access the control systems and view process data remotely.
8. Cybersecurity: This layer includes security solutions and protocols that are used to protect the OT systems and devices from cyber threats. Examples include firewalls, intrusion detection and prevention systems, and security information and event management (SIEM) systems.

17. OT ASSET DISCOVERY AND ASSET MANAGEMENT FUNDAMENTALS & BEST PRACTICE

Operational Technology (OT) Asset Discovery and Asset Management are critical processes for understanding and maintaining the inventory of devices, systems, and software that make up an organization's OT environment. The fundamentals and best practices of OT Asset Discovery and Asset Management include:

1. Inventory management: This involves maintaining an accurate inventory of all the devices, systems, and software that make up the organization's OT environment. This should include information such as device type, manufacturer, model number, location, and IP address.
2. Asset classification: It is important to classify the assets into different categories, such as critical, non-critical, IT and OT to prioritize the protection of critical assets.
3. Network topology mapping: This involves creating a visual representation of the organization's OT network, including all devices, systems, and communications pathways.
4. Vulnerability management: This involves identifying and assessing vulnerabilities in the organization's OT devices and systems, and developing plans to mitigate or eliminate those vulnerabilities.
5. Configuration management: This involves maintaining accurate information about the configuration of the organization's devices and systems, including software versions, patch levels, and security settings.
6. Software management: This involves managing the software that is installed on the organization's OT devices and systems, including patching, updates and inventory.
7. Regularly conduct vulnerability assessments and penetration testing: This involves regularly testing the organization's OT systems and devices for vulnerabilities, and identifying any areas that may need to be improved.

8. Access control management: This involves managing access to the organization's OT devices and systems, including controlling who has access, what access they have, and logging all access attempts.
9. Incorporating security by design principles: This involves designing and implementing security measures from the beginning of the project, throughout its life-cycle.
10. Collaborate with other organizations and industry groups to share threat intelligence and best practices.
11. Have incident response plan in place and regular testing of incident response plans.
12. Evaluating third party vendors and maintaining a robust vendor management program.

18. OT SECURE ACCESS MANAGEMENT

Operational Technology (OT) Secure Access Management refers to the process of controlling and monitoring access to the devices and systems that make up an organization's OT environment. The best practices for OT Secure Access Management include:

1. Authentication: This involves verifying the identity of users who are attempting to access the organization's OT devices and systems, typically through the use of usernames and passwords, digital certificates, or biometric authentication.
2. Authorization: This involves determining what level of access a user should have to the organization's OT devices and systems, based on their role and responsibilities within the organization.
3. Access control: This involves physically or logically controlling access to the organization's OT devices and systems, including the use of security devices such as firewalls, intrusion detection and prevention systems, and VPNs.

4. Least privilege: This involves granting users the minimum level of access necessary to perform their job functions, and revoking access when it is no longer needed.
5. Segregation of duties: This involves separating the responsibilities of different users and groups to prevent any one person from having too much control over the organization's OT systems and devices.
6. Monitoring and logging: This involves monitoring and logging all access attempts to the organization's OT devices and systems, and reviewing the logs regularly to identify and respond to any security incidents.
7. Incident response: This involves having a plan in place to respond to security incidents and regularly testing incident response plans.
8. Remote access management: This involves managing and securing remote access to the organization's OT devices and systems, including the use of VPNs, two-factor authentication, and network segmentation.
9. Third-party vendor access management: This involves managing and securing access

19. OT DISASTER RECOVERY AND BUSINESS CONTINUITY BEST PRACTICE

Disaster recovery and business continuity best practices for operational technology (OT) systems include:

1. Conducting regular risk assessments to identify potential threats and vulnerabilities.
2. Business Impact Analysis (BIA): This involves analyzing the potential impact of a disruption to the organization's operations, including the financial and operational impacts.
3. Disaster recovery planning: This involves developing detailed plans for how the organization will respond to and recover from a disaster or other disruptive event.

4. Business continuity planning: This involves developing plans for how the organization will maintain its operations during and after a disaster or other disruptive event.
5. Data backup and replication: This involves regularly backing up and replicating critical data and systems to ensure that they can be quickly restored in the event of a disaster.
6. Testing and validation: This involves regularly testing and validating the organization's disaster recovery and business continuity plans to ensure that they will work as intended.
7. Incident response planning: This involves having a plan in place to respond to security incidents and regularly testing incident response plans.
8. Developing a comprehensive disaster recovery plan that includes procedures for data backup, restoration, and recovery.
9. Establishing a clear chain of command for decision making and communication during an incident.
10. Regularly testing and updating the disaster recovery plan to ensure its effectiveness.
11. Maintaining off-site backups of critical data and systems to ensure availability in the event of a disaster.
12. Establishing procedures for monitoring and responding to alarms and other indicators of a potential incident.
13. Ensuring that all critical systems and data are protected by appropriate security measures such as firewalls, intrusion detection, and encryption.
14. Providing training and education to all employees on disaster recovery and business continuity procedures.
15. Having agreements and plans in place with outside vendors and service providers to ensure continuity of operations in case of an incident.

16. Continuously monitoring and updating the system and infrastructure to ensure they are running at optimal level.

20. WHAT IS CYBER OPERATIONAL TECHNOLOGY (OT) MONITOR AND MAINTAIN DEFENSES

1. Cyber Operational Technology (OT) monitoring and maintaining defenses refers to the process of monitoring and protecting OT systems from cyber threats. This includes implementing security measures such as firewalls, intrusion detection and prevention systems, and security information and event management (SIEM) systems to detect and respond to potential threats.
2. It also involves continuous monitoring of network traffic and system logs to detect any unusual activity or signs of a cyber attack. This information can be used to identify vulnerabilities and take appropriate action to mitigate them.
3. Regularly updating software and firmware, applying security patches, and applying best practices for secure configuration are also important aspects of maintaining defenses.
4. It also includes identifying, assessing and managing the risks that could impact the availability, integrity, and confidentiality of OT systems, networks and data.
5. In addition, implementing incident response plans, testing and training personnel in incident response procedures and regular drills will help to be prepared in case of a cyber incident.
6. Overall, the goal of OT monitoring and maintaining defenses is to detect and respond to potential threats and vulnerabilities in a timely manner, in order to minimize the risk of a successful cyber attack and protect the availability, integrity, and confidentiality of OT systems and the data they process.

21. BEST PRACTICE FOR ICS IOT AND 5G NETWORK

The integration of Industrial Control Systems (ICS) with the Internet of Things (IoT) and 5G networks brings new challenges for securing these systems. Some best practices for securing ICS, IoT, and 5G networks include:

1. Network Segmentation: Segment the ICS network from the IT network and the IoT network to prevent unauthorized access. This can be achieved by using firewalls, intrusion detection/prevention systems, and network segmentation devices.
2. Monitoring and Logging: Monitor and log all network traffic for suspicious activity, and have an incident response plan in place to quickly identify and respond to security breaches.
3. Access Control: Restrict access to ICS, IoT and 5G network to only authorized personnel and use authentication and encryption to secure communications.

4. Patch Management: Keep software and systems up-to-date with the latest security patches, and have a vulnerability management program in place to identify and address vulnerabilities in a timely manner.
5. Cybersecurity testing: Regularly conduct security audits and penetration testing to identify vulnerabilities and weaknesses in the system.
6. Employee Training: Train employees to be aware of potential security risks and how to identify and report them.
7. Secure by design: Use security by design principles to build secure ICS, IoT, and 5G networks, which focuses on security throughout the life cycle of the system.
8. Use of Secure protocols: Use of secure protocols such as TLS, DTLS, and IPSEC to encrypt communications, and avoid the use of legacy, unencrypted protocols.

It's important to implement a comprehensive security strategy that addresses the unique challenges of securing ICS, IoT, and 5G networks. With the increasing interconnectivity of these systems, it's crucial to ensure they are protected against cyber threats.

Made in United States
Troutdale, OR
11/03/2026

56845099R00024